Waking Hours and Rebirth Days
poetry and musings

By

Marie Walker

To you, tenderhearted, who thought you couldn't survive the long, dark nights.

I meant to write about death, only life came breaking in.

— Virginia Woolf

SILENCE

The Hidden Agony

Early fractures, grief, and the woman in descent.

The unnamed ache

The water is still
and eerily tranquil,
but not perfectly noiseless.
The surface seemingly untouched,
an old well, so hushed.
A leaf could fall,
and I—
kept setting off the ripple's effect.
My mind is a mess—each thought left unchecked,
a helpless call,
I ask why—
why did I let myself be in such distress?

Meanwhile the wind gently blows—
I held my breath. Then I rose.
Jaw clenched against the thought—
of all that the unnamed ache once brought.
I do not speak of it,
no words seem to fully fit.

This night would soon end,
and in the day, I will have to pretend.
Yet the moon, even in its fullness,
confessed, it couldn't ease the sadness
buried deep at the bottom—
where unsaid things, I still cannot fathom—

of this still and eerily tranquil
water of the pit that refuses to spill.
If only it would rain—hours on hours—again,
until the well would overflow and pour out my pain.

What the body cannot forget

What the body cannot forget
finds its way to resurface, surely
follows like a shadow, vague as a silhouette.

'Who is there?' she asked—an imminent threat.
Trembling hands, sweating, it's clear to see
what the body cannot forget.

Taken aback by a sudden noise, she starts to fret.
Huge columns of trees taking on shapes, obscurely
follows like a shadow, vague as a silhouette.

The forest grew darker: grief, anger, and regret—
confused and alarmed but does not know entirely
what the body cannot forget.

What is there to escape from? She doesn't know it yet.
Heart racing with uneasy, pungent smell of anxiety
follows like a shadow, vague as a silhouette.

Down on her knees, sobbing in a montage of needs unmet,
in the middle of a dense woods, despairingly.
What the body cannot forget
follows like a shadow, vague as a silhouette.

Clarity (after Eve)

I need clarity—
am I the bone of your bones,
and flesh of your flesh?
Am I the rib taken from you—
the one a man would name as his?

If you're not the one,
then walk away gently.
I have no time to spare
if your love's just another despair.

I am Eve, but are you my Adam?
I need clarity.
My bones say you may not be,
and my flesh is drawn to yours.

But if I'm not the rib taken from you,
if I'm not the one a man would name his,
then walk away gently.

I have no time to spare
if your love's just another despair.
Yet still I ache for what feels ancient and pure.
Not for control, but for a love that's secure.

I need clarity.
If your love's just despair, then walk away gently.

Yoke

Carrying grief as a map of guidance—into silence,
With footsteps reverberating in tough submission
Into dark valleys, dragging heavily to a distance
Enough to awaken remorse, to arouse contrition.

She breathes the ache as sacred sustenance,
Enough to nourish even the insatiable hunger
For conclusion without building up dissonance
From the naivety; oh, youth full of blunder!

Why must one suffer such grievous atonement—
Despairingly retracing a holistic resonance
Once held before yielding to self-abandonment—
Springing from somebody else's foible arrogance?

You might need some saving, but woman:
Do not lose yourself ruminating in silence.

In the Shape of Absence

I bought flowers more often than before,
And smiled more frequently,
In front of the mirror, to by passers,
Even while I'm lonely.

The birds fly high; nobody really cares.
Somebody, understand,
That after all, I still do wonder if
I'd find a helping hand?

Please bear with me and oh, please be patient.
I know it's getting late,
The sunbeams making way for the twilight,
Still by myself I wait.

Alone, I waited for happier times,
Flowers in hand, smiling.
Life, in the shape of absence, is winter,
I am waiting for spring.

The sky is empty; I'm alone and spiraling down.

The sky is empty; I'm alone and spiraling down.
Keep it inside; keep it hidden. In silence, I suffer.
I try to keep smiling; I try not to frown.

I act as usual and go to town.
Note to self: I need to be tougher.
The sky is empty; I'm alone and spiraling down.

Who am I fooling? I'm such a clown.
But even if navigating this gets rougher,
I try to keep smiling; I try not to frown.

Remember: I am a queen with a crown.
Yet again, I'm a mere bluffer.
The sky is empty; I'm alone and spiraling down.

Keep swimming, try not to drown.
Despite my growth stalling into buffer,
I try to keep smiling; I try not to frown.

The silence whispers truths beneath my gown,
So I take it all off, for there's no need to cover.
The sky is empty; I'm alone and spiraling down.
I try to keep smiling; I try not to frown.

FLAME

Fragments and Ritual

The first spark. A woman begins to gather pieces.

Kindling

She, so beloved—
too great intimacy
echoed in the poet's poems,
with rhymes coming and going
all about her.

She, an enchanting thing—
maiden of love songs
sang in some lonely place.
Within her longs for transformation,
rather than making a dart interruption
as a dead eternity with infinite brief existences.

She, love embodied—
healing touch so tender,
broken heart mender
unpacking true emotions,
unwrapping selves and be true selves.

Inwardly listening to her own rhythm,
following a distinct tempo, tuning and retuning
every so often to feel like herself always and again.
A lady acclimated to the flame within her heart;
a kindling fueling her own.

Ember

Try it and you will know—
one of the few fires
worth the burning.
It's the kind that leaves no mark
upon the skin,
yet its truth starts carving
into the bone,
revealing something from within
that has eventually grown,
that will eventually show.

Don't be ashamed of your own sentimentality
even of your possible love;
what about it that makes it so uneasy?

What remains when all loves were lost?
Emotional remnants that still glow—
would you allow a new spark?
Something still survives after all loves fade.

Ignition

There is no point in projection
If you cannot face the horror
Of your misguided feelings, and twisted thoughts—
Both disturbingly distorted—
Making their way to regression,
Because you cannot bear the weight
Of the inner turmoil brewing
Within the self you so reject.

So you smash the mirror before it speaks,
Pick up the shards and throw false accusations,
While you run over your own reflection
Again and again,
As if that truly makes you feel better
When you know it could not silence the scream.

But anguish, however deeply buried,
Seeps through the cracks, finds its way to the surface,
Wears your name like a foul language,
Haunts you in your sleep.

When you're alone it wakes
And whispers: *you have no escape, for I am you, still.*

Yet you decide—you decide to carry it around
While it slowly gnaws at your own marrow.
Yet you blame—you blame others for your own sorrow

While it sets your shame alight—scorching.

When you're alone it wakes
And whispers: *the only way out is to sit with yourself.*

Ablaze

You intoxicate me—
Sweet yet dangerous wine; red, pressed
Hard against my body
Throughout the night, you are my quest.

Your eyes, bright as the moon,
Light in the dark, captivating
My thirsty heart too soon—
But do you have what I'm seeking?

Forgive me if I stare
Like there's no tomorrow, at you
Who seem quite half-aware
That your beauty's a thrilling view.

In vino veritas:
Skin to skin, now the truth reveals
Itself in bold glory,
Making known what the heart conceals.

Yet for all that, it's vain
To think it is an elixir
To ease and take the pain
When t'was never a quick fixer.

Still, I savor the taste,
Aroma, and texture you give—

Fleeting, but not a waste
Of time; we have this night to live.

Kiss marks shade of crimson:
Love or lust? Do you feel a spark?
Can you find a reason
To stay? I urge you to embark.

Flicker

She could hear a quaver in her whisper:
'Rush! Hush!' on her way out of the forest.
Trapped within its depths, she bushwhacks through, lest
What drowns her own mind catches up to her.
Past thorned thickets, she moved in weak shiver
this weary night must have been the longest.
'Why me? I am not among the strongest.'
She went on until she saw a flicker

Of light. Finally, she sees a clearing
Not too close, but it is neither too far.
And yet, the glade was void of existence
This, for her, have felt blatantly wounding.
Pale crimson, a deep cut without a scar—
Resurging ache of blazing persistence.

Slow Burn

A moment of weakness buried a better judgment six-feet under.
What use does self-recrimination have if one
does not feel remorse?
Tell me the value of a mind full of shame
with a heart absent of guilt.

Cemented heart in a beautiful body;
cemented hearts need to feel sorry.
Although an inch away from weeping, I remained dry-eyed.
And please let me think, alas, I don't want to remember.

…demented soul frightened of what it will become—
what it has become.

I wish you remember what we did last night.

Flares

Drawing my eyes against my will,
something burned in me;
my nerves sang with the danger.
Overwhelmed and helpless—
In seas of tears I float.
This night may never witness the morning,
One night finally won't.

Is there a song more silent than
that of the unspeaking heart?

THE ASCENT TO RECLAMATION

Triptych Chapter

A sacred turning point—mythic, personal, sovereign.

Invocation

for the woman who survived herself

Meet her where she is at—
grieving, unfinished,
smeared with memory and soft with current ache.

Let her bring the silence that's been sitting inside
because no one seemed to listen.
Let her bring the pieces she thought
are too broken to belong.

Here at the table, nothing is wasted.
Her sorrow is sacred.
Even regret finds form.

This is not a return,
but an uprising.
She is not beginning again—
she is becoming.

The Ascent to Reclamation

How much courage did it take to reclaim her?
She grieved, and grieved; but what was she grieving for?
Was it the lost past,
or perhaps, the lost future?
Sit with her for a moment and you will find–
all the despair, anguish, and frustration combined.

Is grief really the price
for loving with all our souls?
By taking a step forward,
she recognized the chain
restraining her movements,
slowing her down.

What must she do, then,
to create progression?
She started by embracing the regrets
that once were the source of doubt
but now, she must learn to accept.

The vision of love she has conceived of–
dancing in the halls of memory,
that at one point gave warmth–
passed like sundrenched days
turned into days shrouded in mist.

She let herself breathe in the scent of bitterness,
You won't know what it's like
unless you've been there.
Reclaiming what's always been hers
means remembering what's always been her:
to honor what was while inviting what may be.

In the quiet of her heart,
she gathers fragments,
pieces of herself scattered
like shards from a broken glass.

And now, what fills the space
where chains once clung?
A mosaic of her former self–
pieced together in freedom, and hopeful light–
serving as an assurance that courage
is not absence of fear,
but a forbearing surrender
where strength is discovered.

It took her enough–
only enough courage to get up and leap in
along the edges of her heart,
finding herself anew.

Bearing in mind
that it's not just a return,
but a daring ascent
toward the life she longs for—
each moment a testament to her rebirth.

Benediction

for the woman who remembered her name

Do not be afraid to go forward—
not perfect, but present.
Not without ache, but with a heart not hardened.

Carry what you've reclaimed:
the sorrow turned seed,
you'll soon reap the quiet resilience that you've sown.

Remain steady at your feet, and tender
even when your hands are shaking.
For you were given the spirit of power.

Let the world forget who you've become—
as long as you remember:
You are not beginning again.
You are becoming—
on your terms,
in your name,
through the light within you.

SALT

The Language of Becoming

A voice unfolded. Identity claimed. Name remembered.

Dinner Party

I sat at the table
And one by one, they all arrived:
Guilt, anger, shame, sadness,
Were the first few to sit with me.

"I wish I knew better,"
Says Guilt, knowing it has been done.
Feeling responsible:
Should have or not have done all that.

Then Anger shouts loudly,
"Why is this happening to me?
This is wrong. It's unfair!
Do something about this or else—"

Shame is ruminating.
Staying quiet, don't want to fight.
"It's out of my control,
I didn't do it; no, not me."

"Maybe these tears would help,"
Sadness couldn't bear it no more.
"Please tell me what to do,
Or else I will be stuck in gloom."

I acknowledged them all.
Then, Shock and Disbelief arrived.
Anxiety soon came,
Along with Confusion and Fear.

The table is now full,

The room felt dark and menacing.
Everybody is here.
It is now my turn to speak up.

"I feel mixed emotions,"
They all reacted uniquely.
"This will be a long night—
We will take all the time we need."

Woman of the new garden

Her name, once chained to ill-bound reliance
Now drifts through hymns of quiet boldness.
Avoiding the temptation of stubborn defiance,
She pursues closure led by thirst for stillness.

A second birth rewriting her story with radiance,
Approaching each chapter with blossomed kindness.
She is finally where love and peace hold alliance,
After a period of walking through the wilderness.

Surely, goodness follows her with newfound deliverance,
As she treads along rows of verdant lushness—
The earth that confirms her deep significance
A woman awake in her new awareness.

Essence

Cycle breaker, acknowledge the role you played.
Hard-pressed, you broke the shell—
unfortunately, yet out of necessity was made;
one you have guarded so well.
Massive disappointment
forced inevitable confrontation.
Evident misalignment
induced inevitable exhaustion.
Trailblazer, wake up to your true essence.
Perplexed, you set yourself free—
without demand, you offer your presence.
This time, only to people who truly see.

Seasoned

Through time, trial and transformation,
you are who you have always been
beneath the armor and shield.

There is healing, and preservation,
as you recognize the purpose
of your identity and voice.

You are here—you have endured.
Everything that you are will soon be restored.
Slow and steady, you prepare for your return.

RETURN

Her Own Homecoming

She re-emerges. No longer searching—now becoming.

Self-Portrait

A mirror that shows too much—
I look but do not see
its desperate attempts at forming
an aqueous, mosaic reflection of me.

Reflecting the bitter touch
of the loser against a lover
who fought heart-on,
who loved and lost;
who is she?
Reminiscent of past selves,
who was she?

A mirror that shows too much—
I look again and finally see
my own desperation at forming
a solid, complete image of me.

My Father's Daughter

Through faded memories, your presence seems to softly echo
A lineage that bound us, a silent but strong connection.
Not many things I remember, but I hold you deep in my heart.
There is a subtle ache shaping unknowingly the patterns of my future,
Deep-rooted, untaught yet learned, molding my sense of identity.
You were supposed to be my very idea of home.

I do remember, warmth and safety, while you were home,
You take my hand, and we dance around—the sound of our laughs echo.
The way you showed up for me, influenced my core identity,
How I yearn for care, love and genuine connection.
I wish I knew what is ahead, what is my future,
All I know is that carry all that you have given me in my heart.

There is no easy way to pinpoint the lingering ache in my heart,
Why I started asking, 'What is home? What is home?'
Slowly but surely, a wound projected onto the future,
Behaviors for survival, and distorted thoughts echo.
The warmth and safety are gone, we have lost the connection,
Lack of stability created a fragmented identity.

The darkness soon came and created a false identity
Resulted from a severed link, followed by a broken heart.
There is no guarantee whether or not we keep our connection,

For the young girl whom I was, lost her home sweet home.
Each night she cries listening to the past that continues to echo,
Each night she asks, 'Where would I be? What would I be in the future?'

There must be, after all, some love waiting for me in the future.
Perhaps, by then, I have acquired a secured identity.
Even when the horrors of the bygone years still echo,
I endured, I have grown, I keep a quiet heart.

The young girl within may be scared still, or longing for a home,
But she is building her community—an intimate, and trusted connection.

We will always be a part of each other: human connection.
I honor the past, live the present, and hope for the future,
When we can be together again, warm, and safe, and home.
I am my father's daughter: that is my identity.
The pain remains, that is true, so I ask for a new heart
That is pure with no fear, and only love, joy, and peace echo.

Here and there, the past might echo, but peace now fills my heart.
My true identity will steadily guide me home
To an eternal future, through a sacred connection.

To the Young Maiden Me

Here's to you, maiden of my former years—
The one I blamed, once or twice,
for wanting too much, for feeling too deep,
for challenging paradigms that betrayed your truth.

I see now: you were only trying to become.

Life wasn't as ideal as you imagined—
not the world, not the people around you,
not even yourself.

You kept reaching—undeniably—
Toward a version of womanhood
Shaped by the standards you quietly self-imposed.

Ego? No.

You were simply born to envision your potential—
whether you never live to witness yourself arrive.

Renascence

Is it loneliness?

What echoes in your head
when you think of her
in teenage years
is she lamenting?

You have done it differently.

You have since learned to get back up
when life trips you over.

Some decisions set limitations.
Some decisions simply have outcomes.

You have lived differently.

You are no longer the princess of the grey chateau.

You are no longer sighing in rumination.

You are in a revival.

LIGHT

Mirrors and Acts of Service

Reflecting joy, love, and peace. Blooming in grace

Sunrises

Orange hues,
soothe my blues.
My days are dreary—
end this misery.

Oh, help me see
I could be free—
finally awake
despite the soft ache.

Breezy waves—
what fate still paves
through life's ebb and flow
keep helping me grow.

Streaks of warm light,
what a delight!
Life remained the same—
look who I became.

Through the window

Sunbeam—

a moment of grace slipping in gently,

entering this phase of my journey

bringing me a sweet, warm gleam.

Glimmer—

a miracle caught mid-breath, unannouncing

its arrival—things I've subtly been waiting

carry a soft, mellow shimmer.

Morrow—

arises after a dark night

permeating a golden light

through the window.

Incandescent

You are the agony that refuses remedy—
Inconsolable.

I love you so much so that I burn for you:
For everything that makes your heart beat,
For everything that brings you joy,
For whatever stirs up your heart,
For whatever makes you feign a smile,
May I be able to attune with you.

If I could find a panacea of misery,
Then I would go through the journey—
No matter how arduous, bitter, or winding
The road to finding it may seem—
Of discovering anything that offers cure.
I love you so much so I burn for you.

Let me be the euphoria that offers remedy—
Incandescent.

Looking-glass

Self-encounter
reveal identity shaped by
all factors you can think of.
Glass of truth,
device of revelation—
not only reflects,
but translates reflection
back to oneself.
Foggy gaze,
a veil,
smoke and mirrors;
deceitful being
abhor confrontation.
Looking-glass
captures light:
portal crossing thresholds
and identity reclaimed quietly.

TEMPLE

Her Pursuit of Life

She is a vessel—a channel of life's intricacies.
Transcendent.

Woman

I call myself a poet
of unwritten thoughts,
and unspoken emotions
against the battle of love
that by now I should know
does not conquer all.

I call myself a lover
but frequently fights
for what her love's worth,
in all my justification
for the decisions I willed
that by now I should know
must be self-righteousness.

I don't call myself a saint
for staying in places
I should already have long left,
although, I seem to be walking
in the paths of martyrdom
that by now I should know
I have been a sacrificial victim
for the glory of love.

In the end, I call myself a woman
with a profound capacity for affection,
a vessel for the divine,
and for the ideals of intimacy
that sometimes get perverted—
a reflection of my humanity.

Life-bearer

As the gibbous moon progressively wanes,
a determined heart releases the reins—
allowing, giving herself the liberty
to bring herself a moment's felicity.

Horizontal lights from the window blinds
the only glow illuminating within the confines
of the room where two become one—
the vessel that she is: spilling's begun.

Make her a channel of love for love's sake,
offering without demand, let the brave one partake.
Make her a channel of pleasure for pleasure's sake,
presenting without condition, what could be at stake?
Make her a channel of comfort for comfort's sake,
understanding without defense, relieved from any ache.

The bearer of life pouring herself out, is ready to transform.
She holds space for surrender—to see and be seen.
She carries the story of desire, grief, hope, endless storm
of tribulations where memories, secrets and scars convene.

The momentary bliss etched its mark eternal.
Temptation or obedience, a decision inertial.

MUSINGS

matters of the heart

Learning how to fully receive affection without questioning it or wondering what the catch is isn't always that easy for someone who's used to having to earn even the slightest bit of love. It can be difficult because it means unlearning the survival instinct of bracing for impact—the ingrained belief that something negative must be waiting around the corner whenever things start to feel a little too good. It can be tough because it means honoring not only the gesture of giving but also honoring one's own worth. It can be challenging because it means learning to trust not only others, but, most importantly, oneself.

I hope to learn to stop anticipating harm in order to feel safe.

So you have loved, you have lost, and yet you choose to love again. Consider yourself courageous. Not everyone can bring themselves to open their hearts once more after being broken, especially with the awareness of the risks that love entails—including the painful ones. You know it isn't as naïve or reckless as you convince yourself in moments of fear; it takes a certain kind of understanding, and it is intentional. It is a profound journey you can embark on as many times as you need, one that carries you far beyond the mundane of daily life.

Choose to believe in love even in moments when it doesn't feel like something worth believing in.

I finally made peace with my own shadows; finally feel less isolated within my own being. I finally understood my complexity, my multifacetedness, and now feel more comfortable to be witnessed as I am. I finally realized I didn't have to dim or shrink myself so as not to disrupt other people's level of comfort. I finally realized that showing up as my authentic self is a boundary I owe to myself.

I am reclaiming my space, voice, and presence.

I refuse to abandon myself again.

Let go of the old versions of yourself—outdated mindsets, behaviors, habits, and patterns—and step into who you're becoming and take what you're meant to receive. Learn not to stand in the way of your own blessing. Be willing to claim what's yours without mistrust. Release control and look forward. Avoid carrying past emotions into new experiences. Don't cloud the current of peace with fear, rather, steady it with love. Let yourself form something even without seeing its full extent. Let life reveal itself in motion.

Would you rather cling to the familiar that doesn't serve you?

A love that agrees to undergo transformation—learning, healing, and growing together; one that doesn't only take from you but also fills you up; one that doesn't make you pull away from yourself but helps you feel safe enough to be authentic. A love that may bring up memories of wounding yet helps recognize the aspects of yourself that were lost and find them again. A love that breaks the constructs that keep one small and creates a space for the active decision to choose oneself, time and again.

This is the kind of love I'd like to nurture.

I am allowing myself to rest as I learn to come out of survival mode. Reframing the tendency toward hyperawareness—that arises when I start thinking I'm doing something wrong—is still a challenge. Shifting my focus to what I've done well— recognizing my strengths rather than giving in and feeding self-sabotaging thoughts—still takes a whole lot of courage and patience. I am learning to trust myself more, healing, and growing a gentle sense of internal safety. There is no rush, only consistency. There is no guilt, only honoring myself worthy of care.

I am giving myself grace as I restore the balance of my being.

Out of self-compassion, do not let other people's lack of capacity to handle you to make you feel like you are too much—the shame is on them. You are allowed to take up space. Some people simply do not have the container for the fullness of love you have to offer—the fullness of your existence.

For someone who has always lived with an open heart despite letdowns, it's awe-inspiring how your heart stays soft and still chooses to open again and again.

Forgive yourself for not realizing sooner that you don't have to lose parts of yourself in the process of loving. Let those anticlimaxes strengthen your mind and allow the softening of your body to naturally unfold. Make it a practice to learn from experience. As certain truths reveal themselves, learn to hold space for both light and darkness. Discover new ways to show up for others—and especially for yourself. You're far stronger and more capable than you give yourself credit for. Not everyone can step into the unknown with the hope that things will slowly align and fall into place.

You're still able to love because love resides within you.

Sometimes it's easier to keep things to ourselves because we think others wouldn't understand anyway. It's easier to stay silent because vulnerability started to feel like a gamble with the risk of being dismissed, minimized, or misunderstood. There is a level of truth to this—not everyone has the patience or emotional capacity to meet us where we are at. But how do we feel less afraid to let them try?

It's when we let others show us who they are. Then we are able to choose the people who make the risk feel worth it. It's when we learn that fear is different from intuition. It's when we build trust that grows from evidence, not hope or potential. It's when we give ourselves permission to open intentionally, and only where there are respect and reciprocity.

They say actions speak louder than words, and perhaps they do.
Yet I've come to realize that actions speak more clearly when
they align with what we say — when the doing and the saying
echo the same truth. You will know they truly love you when
they can reject the impulse to indulge in their violent nature
and replace it with gentleness. You will know it by the way they
hold space for you—safe, genuine, and present.

Allow others to show up for you as much as you show up for them.

It's a futile attempt to escape oneself—we cannot disembark from ourselves. It's a constant revolt against our past and new selves to be who we are in the present. So, whether the cup is half empty or half full, at the end of the day, we are who we decide we are. Ultimately, we will learn that we are insatiable beings, that others have little to do with our pursuit of validation, and that one of the very few things we can do to bring about our own happiness is to fill up our own cups. In doing so, we can no longer blame others for our unhappiness. Isn't it a massive relief that we no longer need other's permission to be happy?

Indeed, wherever we go, there we are.

Perhaps the happy ending can look like:

a calm nervous system.

the kind that no longer flinches at every memory of what once
hurt you,
the kind that understands peace is not a luxury but a quiet
battle we choose daily;

unrushed mornings.

where sunlight filters through the window
and you finally have the space to hear your own breath,
to stretch into the day at your own pace;

remaining as the soft, loving person that you are,

despite how the world has been toward you,
because you've learned that softness is not a weakness—
it's where your strength lives,
as a way of staying true to yourself.

Maybe the happy ending is simply this:

a life that no longer demands you to put on armor to survive,
a life where you can move slowly, love deeply,
and live in a way that feels true to you.

Epilogue

Returning to oneself is not a destination—
it is a living ritual.

Author Reflection

On the Sacredness of Grief, Memory and the Voice of Womanhood

I did not arrive at these poems neatly. They came to me scattered—in vague fragments.

Most feelings are certainly fleeting, yet there are those that stay under the surface. There are those that I scream for time: to heal, to vanish, to be taken out of my system. Grief still lingers in the corners of my memory, suppressed in silence, wrapped in a linen cloth that I mistook for healing and obedience.

This collection of poetry and musings is surely not about mastering pain but about sitting with oneself, being one's own listener born out of necessity and of permission. It is not at all comfortable. It is almost as if you are meeting yourself to be interrogated and bombarded with questions that you are not even sure how to ask in the first place. It is awkward but necessary if one intends to pursue healing.

Grief, for me, is shaped in sacredness. For in grief, I found intimacy with myself—to care for, to deeply cherish, to forgive, to protect. It is when I found myself in a place of desperation that I cried out to the divine for help. Grief must be inviolable—so as not to be devoured, then numb.

Here, memory is not a map back to the lived-out tribulations, but a thread leading toward reclamation. It is not to revisit and wound anew. Rather, memory is there to reminisce, to treasure, or maybe to simply be pondered upon. There are memories I hope to stay with me for as long as I live, there are some that I just want to fade away immediately. But no matter how these memories look for each of us, the certain kinds of memories we tend to circle back to are the ones that shape our becoming.

On the other hand, womanhood is not merely a role, but a rite. A solemn act. A transition period. If I return to Eve, it is not to blame or romanticize. It is to sit beside her—spirit to spirit, bones to bones, and heart to heart—and ask: *What did you lose after you've been told you lost everything you had?*

I offer these pages not as a resolution, but as a liturgy for those still remembering, still stitching themselves back together from the shadow of a downcast spirit.

Acknowledgment

This book was conceived as an act of acceptance—a response to the calling to write, guided by a deep sense that I was meant to share my story.

I would like to express my heartfelt gratitude to everyone who supported me throughout the creation of this book. Your encouragement, presence, and belief in my gift carried me through every stage of this journey.

To the early readers who welcomed and met these poems before they were in their final state—thank you for your care, patience, thoughtful feedback, and support.

Special thanks to: *Dianne, Zephyr, Abigail, Hannah, Jaz, Rei, Trish, Tina, Rachel, et al.*

To my friends and family, thank your for celebrating the small victories. To those whose conversations, kindness, or quiet encouragement sparked inspiration throughout these pages— I am grateful for the ways you helped shape this book without even realizing it.

To my muse, whose existence grounds me and reminds me that this gift is worth pursuing.

And finally, to every reader who finds something of themselves in these words: thank you. It is an honor to share this space with you. You are loved.

About the Author

Marie Walker is a poet and writer whose work drifts through themes of love and loss, introspection, light and darkness, and inner worlds we rarely speak aloud. She draws inspiration from nature, the complexities of the human heart and mind, and the lived experiences that shape us.

When she's not writing, she can be found savoring her coffee, reading, daydreaming, enjoying her solitude, or collecting moments and memories. She believes in the power of poetry to heal, grow, and connect with readers on a deeper, more human level.